Kenson was a curious little boy with a big smile and even bigger dreams. Every day felt like a new adventure! Today, he was ready for his biggest adventure yet – a day exploring the park with his mom.

"Are you ready, Kenson?" his mom asked. "Ready!"
Kenson said, grabbing his favorite red hat.

As they walked to the park, Kenson saw a fluffy dog across the street. "Mom! Look at the dog!" he said, running toward it.

But Mom quickly held his hand. "Wait, Kenson! Remember, we need to stop and look both ways before crossing the street."

Kenson stopped, and they looked left, then right, then left again. No cars were coming, so they safely crossed the street together.

"Wow, Mom! That's how we stay safe when we cross the street, right?" Kenson asked.

"That's right, Kenson!" she said with a smile.
"Always look both ways."

When they got to the park, Kenson ran straight for the playground. There was a big slide he couldn't wait to try. As he started to climb the ladder, his mom called out, "Kenson, remember to hold on tight with both hands!"

Kenson grabbed the rails and climbed carefully. When he got to the top, he felt proud. "I'm being safe, Mom!" he called down.

As Kenson slid down, he felt the wind rush on his face. "Wheee!" he laughed. When he reached the bottom, he saw some kids playing near the swings.

"I want to swing, too!" Kenson shouted.

But as he started to run toward the swings, his mom reminded him, "Kenson, be careful! We don't run too close to swings. Someone could bump into you."

Kenson looked around and noticed the kids on the swings were moving fast. He waited until the swings stopped, then he joined in.

After lots of fun at the park, Kenson saw a
friendly squirrel by the big oak tree. "Can I pet
the squirrel, Mom?" he asked.

Mom shook her head. "It's important to be safe around animals we don't know, Kenson. Wild animals like squirrels might be scared and could bite."

Kenson nodded. "I'll just wave hello to the squirrel from here!"

As the day came to an end, Kenson and his mom started walking home. They passed by a big group of kids playing tag.
"Can I join them, Mom?" Kenson asked.

"You can, but stay where I can see you," Mom reminded him. "It's always good to stay close to a grown-up so you don't get lost."

Kenson played with the kids but kept an eye on his mom the whole time. He felt happy and safe.

When they finally got home, Kenson gave his mom a big hug. "Today was the best adventure ever!" he said.

"And you did such a great job staying safe!" his mom replied. "You looked both ways when crossing the street, held on tight at the playground, stayed away from wild animals, and stayed close to me."

Kenson smiled proudly. "I'm going to be safe on every adventure from now on!"

Mom kissed his forehead and said, "That's my brave, smart boy."

That night, Kenson drifted off to sleep with dreams of more big adventures – always remembering to stay safe along the way.

The End

Kenson's Safety Tips:

1. Always look both ways before crossing the street.

2. Hold on tight when climbing or playing.

3. Stay away from wild animals.

4. Stay close to a grown-up in new places.

5. Have fun, but always remember to be safe!